SHORES
COMPENDIUM OF POEMS

DR. SEEKU CLELAND

Compendium of Poems
Copyright © 2025 by Dr. Seeku Cleland.

All rights reserved. No part of this publication may be reproduced, distributed, or transmitted in any form or by any means, including photocopying, recording, or other electronic or mechanical methods, without the written consent of the publisher. The only exceptions are for brief quotations included in critical reviews and other noncommercial uses permitted by copyright law.

MILTON & HUGO L.L.C.
4407 Park Ave., Suite 5
Union City, NJ 07087, USA

Website: *www. miltonandhugo.com*
Hotline: *1- 888-778-0033*
Email: *info@miltonandhugo.com*

Ordering Information:
Quantity sales. Special discounts are granted to corporations, associations, and other organizations. For more information on these discounts, please reach out to the publisher using the contact information provided above.

Library of Congress Control Number:		2025903021
ISBN-13:	979-8-89285-425-2	[Paperback Edition]
	979-8-89285-426-9	[Hardback Edition]
	979-8-89285-427-6	[Digital Edition]

Rev. date: 06/09/2025

Contents

Shores 1
Maiden 2
Pitter-Patter 3
Gridlock 4
Relationships 5
What the Heart Knows 6
666 9
Tortured Soul 11
Cancel Culture 13
The Stone that the Builder Refused 16
Call me Imhotep 17
The Disbelievers the Wicked 19
Second Glance 20
Route 66 22
911 27
Lock the Doors 33
Social Media 35
Where are weapons of Mass Destruction 38
An Inconvenient Truth 42
Pour Libation 45

Shores

The ambient noise of the ocean's
crashing waves beckon straddling
walkers along white sandy beaches
hearts gaze wistfully beyond
hills of distant horizons
horizons clouded by fading
sunsets as rays of hope dart past a
darkening sun the sun casts its
dragnet along
twisting weathered promontories
as star-crossed lovers whisper
excitedly Sirius the brightest star
quickly signals its retreat

Maiden

a furtive glance cast by a fair maiden
maiden blissfully unaware of her
power to move imagination
imaginations that lay bare prose
prose that has neither rhyme nor reason
reason that modulates oscillations
of fluttering hearts
hearts that gaze upon a distant horizon
the horizon of the city of Ellicott
Ellicott punctuated by swiveling lamps
that guide approaching ships
ships weary of perilous breakwaters
breakwaters that protect against the crashing and
eroding waves
waves that shield a galloping and
deepening darkness
a darkness that hides a shifting fog
fog that blankets eroding banks
banks of the city of Ellicott

Pitter-Patter

it startles somnolent
slobberers the incessant
pitter-patter
of drum rolls that accompany
the heavy pelting of raindrops
against poorly insulated windows
and eaves in bed children and
adults shift wistfully the reverie
luring them to contemplate this
unwelcome interruption
meanwhile insomniacs stretch
weary limbs as they yank the last
few yards of blankets over cold
torsos hope lingers for a concluding
stint to this unending cycle of
sounds, shapes, and images of REM
and non-REM dreams without
warning, the clarion call of alarm
bells startle rip van winkles from
their boundless cacophony of dreams

Gridlock

it takes over your senses when the
inevitable turn is made the
length of the gridlock
provokes a nuanced thought
thoughts we do not fully understand
that we are pawns in a large chess
game, a chess game controlled by a force
a hidden force that pushes and pulls
on our senses careers and children's
schooling
the invisible hand
this hand that sways the pendulum
controls the trajectory
of our careers
this imperious hand has the power to
calculate our time to retirement and whisper
if our children will become forever-dependents
or self-sustaining this majestic hand keeps us
company into the twilight of our existence
and helps us accept the verisimilitude once
we have a moment of clarity
that each passing birthday brings us
closer to our inevitable destination
one chosen by the eternal hand
the hand of Fatima that determined the
moment of our conception and foretold
the last few miles of our final destination

Relationships

relationships mimic organisms
and take on static or dynamic
evolutionary cycles
dynamic relationships blossom so
communication lines remain
open, and expressions of affection
are reciprocated and, whether
static or dynamic
relationships take on
a predictable pattern
relationships speak to the human
condition they mimic the life cycle of a moth
as organisms become extinct,
and relationships die

What the Heart Knows

what the heart knows the
a mind has not yet grasped
it comes upon you slowly
a realization that something
within you is broken and cannot
be fixed
it is akin to the creeping of an
apex predator
stealthily stalking its prey
this fractured emotion
consumes you like an erupting volcano
makes your heart jump into your
mouth when you come across the
object of your affection
you begin to question your sanity
not understanding your fight or flight
responses wondering why you have
become easily excitable to that of a child
expecting a big Christmas present Your
obsession keeping you up at night
Making you question what has come over
you Until suddenly and without warning
you perceive a flickering light
a flickering light in a dark tunnel
and you suddenly accept what has
become obvious to everyone
the observers who bore witness

to your capitulation
and whispered what they had
witnessed
that the arc of history
bends towards love

Prologue

The identity of the Antichrist has long baffled historians and prognosticators. Even the great Nostradamus waded into the debate with the publication of his Quatrains.

666

John Kennedy could not
avoid the assassin's
bullet
Robert Kennedy could not
escape the assassin's bullet
Martin Luther King did not
see the assassin's bullet
666 saw the assassin's
bullet, but it only
grazed him
666 straddled a golden
escalator
in a bid for the American
Presidency, the color of his
hair matched the color of the
escalator
a sketch forever seared
into the collective
consciousness
evoking images of a golden Oscar
666 had *The Apprentice*
666 supporters refer
to him as Orange Jesus
666 designates the sign
of the beast
666 was prophesied by
the Apostle Paul

666 a man of lawlessness
666 the Apostle John
identified as the antichrist
666 the bible illuminated
how his end will occur
666 whom the Lord will
destroy by the breadth of his
mouth

Tortured Soul

O thou tortured soul
knoweth thee not that God
judgeth not his creation?
knoweth thee not that one
must always follow one's
heart?
knoweth thee not that one
cannot Predetermine who
one loves?
knoweth thee not that the
most important outcome
for the soul is serenity?
O tortured soul, dost thou not
know
that when the contents of the
graves are poured forth that what
is hidden in men's hearts will be
made manifest?
O, tortured soul, dost thou not
know that thy Lord has been well
acquainted with thee from the
moment of inception?
O, tortured soul, does thou not
know that I will always be your
friend?
O, tortured soul, do thou not
know that I will always be your

friend?
O, tortured soul do not hide
behind a label. thy Lord judgeth
thee not and neither do I

Cancel Culture

Black and Brown success is transitory
subject to cancel culture
examples countless names
never ending
O.J. Simpson, Michael
Jackson, Bill Cosby,
Kobe Bryant
Ron Artest
R. Kelly, Meghan Markle
Idris Alba, Michelle Obama
Will Smith, Ray Rice
Jay Z, Kanye West
Puff Daddy, Aziz Ansari
Chrissy Teigen Hasan Minhaj
Dixie Chicks
the names run like the
credit section of a movie clip
except it is real life
this farce has swallowed famous
athletes, musicians, politicians, even
movie stars
social influencers across
the political spectrum
who fended one or more
stakeholders in the public space
pilloried by the mainstream media who
not long ago, had built them up as

paragons of virtue overnight and
without warning they were
metamorphosed into
social pariahs
lacking in core moral values
whenever opportunities presented
themselves, we did not stand up for
them as members if our communities
it was more important to be accepted
by the collective group and to
dutifully remain silent
some Blacks even engaged in
public lampooning, goaded by a mob
a mob with a crab mentality
mirroring mankind's biblical
fall from grace reminded
through social media how our
Black and Brown heroes
had fallen from grace
after having committed
one or more of the poet
Dante Alighieri's sins
detailed in his classic
The Divine Comedy
Dante completed his journey
through the nine concentric
circles of Hell

the analogy is our Black and
Brown heroes must similarly
complete this journey if they are to
be saved as custodians of the truth
we must collectively undertake
this journey to obtain the
catharsis and absolution Dante
sought in *Paradise Lost*
Dante initially descended through
Hell (the recognition of sin)
then ascended through purgatory
(the renunciation of sin)
Dante ultimately achieved
the pinnacle of joy
(saw the light of God)
During the final chapter of
Paradise Redeemed
Dante's journey is a metaphor for the
obstacle-strewn highways we encounter
on our discovery of salvation
these struggles are vividly
illustrated in *The Divine Comedy*

The Stone that the Builder Refused

Alif Laam Meem (A.L.M.)
three mysterious consonants
of the Holy Quran
understood only by he that
was present at creation
Lord God, creator of the heavens and
the earth and all that is seen and unseen
everything created on earth belongeth
to him
yet the builder cast aside stones
mankind is ungrateful
when his Lord bleseth
him with riches he sayeth
my Lord hath blessed me
but when his Lord trieth him
he says my Lord has abandoned me
Lo with hardship goeth ease
Lo again with hardship goeth ease
so, when thou art relieved
still toil and strive to please
thy Lord
remember that the stone the builder
refused shall be the
head cornerstone

Call me Imhotep

call me Imhotep
Vizier to Djoser
first king of the third dynasty
of Egypt
I came in peace
I built massive grain silos in a
time of abundance
and together with the biblical
Joseph, saved the people of
Egypt during the Seven-year
drought
Moses had been warned Pharaoh
about I conceived the pyramids
at Giza in Memphis when a
vision fell upon me as I slept
along the banks
of the Nile River over 4600
years ago A vision to build
pyramids
pyramids to house
the souls of the departed
Pharaohs, the souls aptly
named Ka and Ba
on their final journey to the
afterlife,
my talents are God-given
my mission foretold

my means fortuitous
my inspiration divine
I embark on
seraphic undertakings
so, do call me Imhotep
whenever you see me
fulfilling the Lord's wishes

The Disbelievers the Wicked

sic... "Frowned and turned away..."
(Quran 80:1-2)
when the messenger of God came
onto them for counsel
sic..." whoever is an enemy to God,
and His angels, and His messengers,
and (so) Gabriel, and Michael,
(should know that) God is surely
an enemy to the unbelievers..."
(Surah 2: Verse: 98).
as for the quaint
unto them thou
showeth regard, yet it is
not their concern if they
grow not in grace
the love of God draweth
believers closer to the light
beware the darkness that
confronts mankind
beware the darkness perchance
that darkness devoureth
believers as skillfully as it does
the disbelievers the wicked

Second Glance

it jolts your mind the way the sight of
a beautiful woman forces you
to take a second glance
the encounter evoked images of the most
perfectly proportioned woman
my eyes had been fortunate to behold
a woman I once met at a bank in Ghana
except this is not a tale about
another chance encounter
with a seductress but rather
a trip on a railway carriage
that was similarly well designed
with vivacious curves
this marvel this carriage
did not have graffiti
nor did it have rank odors
the kind that uninvitingly perforates
your 5 senses on New York City
subways
except this time, I was not in New York
but rather Abu Dhabi
a faraway Middle Eastern country
presently, as I waited my turn
on its clean platform
I beheld a rapidly approaching
train carriage that looked
unoccupied

so, I willingly boarded
only to realize that the
occupants were all female
I'd failed to make that initial
cultural connection
until I realized only too late
that all eyes were on me
I quickly regrouped and pulled
out my iPhone
having battled for the
past three days
the withering effects
of my room's air conditioner
but suddenly, without warning
a lone black beauty in a sea of white
faces belted out in a plaintive voice that
I had to move to an adjoining male
carriage so next time you fly out to the
Middle East, be sure
to be cognizant of their Islamic
cultural traditions

Route 66

Route 66
immortalized in American
consciousness Celebrated in film
commemorated in song
honored in literature
depicted in John Steinbeck's
Grapes of Wrath,
John Steinbeck exalted Route 66
as the *"Mother Road"*
Route 66 is engraved on tee shirts
and general merchandise
memorialized in the naming of
restaurants Restaurant names
include:
Dot Route 66
Route 66 Diner
Hwy 66 Diner
Flo's 66 Diner
Nowhere on Route 66
Route 66 symbolized
Freedom
Route 66 caters to car lovers
Route 66 epitomizes mobility
Route 66 conjures images of a lost
time A time when the world was
smaller,
a time when school children wore

uniforms, a time when mothers
stayed at home
a time when fathers went to work,
a time when families sat together
for dinner
a time when families had
conversations during mealtimes
when families were more cohesive
a time when *Coke* was the
number one drink
a time when TV was black and white
a time when New York had
only three TV stations
a time when cell phones did not exist
a time when one needed a nickel to
place a call on a public phone
a time when American cars were
extreme gas guzzlers
a time when a gallon of gas
cost 25-30 cents
a time before America's wars with Asia
that era now extant
not many understand the
origins of Route 66
not many comprehend that
Route 66 was established in 1926
not many appreciate that Route 66

was one of the first highways
in the U.S.
not many recognize that the
U. S. Highway System was a
major exit point for families
escaping the 1930s Dust Bowl
not many appreciate
Route 66 cris-crosses
Illinois, Missouri, Kansas
not many accept Route 66
passes through Oklahoma,
Texas, New Mexico
not many people know
Route 66 bisects Arizona
and California
not many know that the
endpoint of Route 66 is Santa
Monica, CA
scarcely any acknowledge that
Route 66 has stunning scenery
hardly any perceive that
Route 66 boasts historic
landmarks

scarcely any realize that a
visit to the Grand Canyon
exposes one to breathtaking
beauty
so, the next time you
trek Route 66, deliberate on
your odyssey so you can fully
appreciate Route 66

Prologue:

Few events in American history have had as severe an impact on the national psyche as 9-11, also known as September 11, 2001. A lack of information sharing between those tracking terrorists at home (FBI) and those tracking terrorists abroad (CIA) created fertile ground for our enemies to launch a bold strike, the likes of which had never been seen and will never be repeated post-mortem.

911

the terrorists designed an enigma that
foretold the date of the 9-11 attack as
September 11, 2001. The enigma goes
as follows
two sticks, a dash, and a cake with a
stick down. What is it
two sticks represent the number 11
a cake with a stick down constitutes the
number 9
the attacks would occur on 11-9
September 11
the number 19
codes for 19 al-Qaeda hijackers
the number 4
cipher for the 4 targets of the attacks
a time when airport security was lax
passengers could carry box cutters
and knives
there were no mandatory ID checks
no *Do Not Fly* lists
passengers could walkthrough
metal detectors without removing their shoes
passengers could carry any
type of liquid onboard
airport security did not
properly check luggage
the cockpit doors were not secure

passengers could access cockpits
the country was not secure
so, the terrorists pounced
they obtained instrument ratings for
flying, except terrorists only trained to
take off
did not acquire instrument ratings
to land a plane
alarm bells should have gone off
intelligence agencies should have
compared notes
each intelligence agency
operated in a glass cocoon
protected themselves from the
real world
and so, we paid the price
the sight of planes slicing through the
North and South Towers
of the World Trade Center
like a knife through butter
Firefighters entrusted with saving lives
we were haunted by the sight of
firefighters climbing up staircases Of
the Twin Towers
to embrace death
even as we watched this tragedy
we wondered

if we were participants
in an alternate reality
wondered if the sight of people
holding hands while jumping
to their deaths
was make-believe
we wondered because we became
childlike and entranced in a
horror movie we could not escape
the distressing sight of the Twin Towers
collapse
the blinding speed of the collapse
breathtaking
we could not take our eyes
off the screen
we could not comprehend
that our world
the world as we knew it
had in one fell swoop
been obliterated
we cried for America
mourned we did
the America we knew
and longed for
belonged to a time
gone by
America, the land of freedom

policeman of the world
was no more
why did the world
hate us so much
that some would fly planes
into buildings
yet, oh yes
America is resilient
America built the 911 Memorial
the 911 Memorial honors
over 3000 lives lost
America did not include
the 19 hijackers
the 19 hijackers who sought martyrdom
we did deny them their martyrdom
we rebuilt the Twin Towers
also called the Freedom Tower
Freedom Tower stands at 1776 feet
1776 is also the year of
America's independence
America is the land of the free
America stands for liberty
America personifies
the Scales of Justice
America is resilient
America outwitted King George
America defeated the British

in the war of independence
America survived Pearl Harbor
in 1942
America defeated Japan
in 1945
America defied Hitler
America sent Hitler
to his suicide in 1945
America will not be cowed
America will not be silenced
America knows that terror never wins
America understands that
the arc of the moral universe
bends toward justice
America takes comfort that
when faced with adversity
"Our flag was still there..." (Key, 1814)

Prologue

It took only 73 seconds for 7 crew members to be forever immortalized in the national discourse. The Columbia disaster occurred more than 40 years ago, on February 01, 2003. NASA was under pressure to launch as many as 25 missions yearly to justify its expensive budget. The event depicted occurred during George H.W. Bush's 41st U.S. presidency.

Lock the Doors

it befell the nation on February 01,
2003. NASA forever tainted
George Herbert Walker Bush President
then on takeoff "...insulating foam from
Columbia's external propellant tank
Struck leading edge of the left wing..."1
of Columbia
Mission Control assessed damage
and ruled damage minimal
crew notified at the last minute
Mission control assured Columbia
reentry safe
Columbia returned from space on
February 01, 2003
the whole country exuberant
nation glued to TV sets
expecting to see Columbia
touchdown in Florida
Columbia is finally visible on screen
flames engulf Columbia
Columbia explodes
parts of aircraft t flying in
different directions
contrails visible all over
took all of 73 seconds
7 lives forever yanked
families perpetually destroyed

NASA assumed 25 ascents
budget massively bloated
schemed they did
prioritized political expediency
over safety
critical design flaws masked
heat shields protect the capsule
heat shields failed
where is contingency plan
fiery phenomenon
spaceships compresses air on reentry
flames are always visible on reentry
flames engulfed aircraft
occupants incinerated
the final order from Houston Mission
control when a mission is in recovery
phase due to catastrophic failure
and when all hope is lost
an accident investigation is
imminent and a need to
preserve accident data
because all lives are lost
"...Lock the Doors..."2

Social Media

Prologue

Social media is a broad term for websites and applications that focus on collaboration. It is noteworthy that while China restricts its social media for its teenagers to math and science, the United States has no such restrictions due to its preference for freedom of expression.

resolves *Algorithms*
dawdles *Time*
foretells *Lower test scores*
inclines *Distraction in class*
occupies *Gaming during class*
effects on *Student Participation Rates*
encourages *Sexting*
procreates *Blackmail*
propagates *Anxiety*
triggers *Depression*
perturbs *Mental health*
stimulates *Pornography*
encounters with
Body Image Issues
battles *Anorexia
nervosa*
fights *Bulimia*
confrontation with *Cyberbullying*
begets *High teen suicide*
effects *Election Interference*
engenders *Misinformation*
so,
Who wins, the United States or China?

Prologue

America never completely recovered from 9-11. That tragedy set in motion a sequence of events that eventually led to the invasion of Iraq, then under the leadership of a former CIA agent, and ruthless dictator, Sadam Hussein. The purpose of the invasion, according to the Bush administration, was to rid Iraq of weapons of mass destruction (nuclear weapons) even though there was heated debate at the time about the wisdom of an invasion, since there was inconclusive evidence that Sadam Hussein had nuclear weapons. The United States went ahead anyway and invaded Iraq. On March 19, 2003, the United States launched "Operation Iraqi Freedom."

Where are weapons of Mass Destruction

face of deceit
Secretary of State Colin Powell
Operation Desert Storm
American hero
highly respected
why art thou here
United Nations Security Council
February 05, 2003
PowerPoint presentation
UNSC Resolution 1441
Iraq (Mesopotamia) is out of compliance 1
Mesopotamia *"Cradle of Civilization" 2*
Mesopotamia has chemical and
biological weapons of mass destruction (nuclear)
March 19, 2003
"Shock and awe" invasion began
early morning hours
overwhelming force
minimal resistance
mass surrenders
Saddam Hussein in hiding
Mesopotamia government collapses
where are weapons of mass destruction
Iraqi museums looted
national treasures gone forever
Salaam Hessen statue toppled
mass jubilations in streets

Baath party banned
Baath party members mostly Sunni
United States declaration
members of Baath party cannot be
part of new interim government
massive unemployment of Sunnis
fateful error
where are weapons of mass destruction
United States pumping billions
bringing democracy to Middle East
mass looting of government coffers
Shiite turn on Sunni majority
against minority
civil war, mass casualties
does the United States understand
understand the religious
and cultural underpinnings
should the United States step
Saddam Hussein captured in manhole
looked unkempt, yet identified himself
as President of Iraq
President hiding in manhole
soldiers laughed and mocked him
where are weapons of
mass destruction?
Donald Rumsfeld could never answer
so many lives lost

so many maimed casualties
where are weapons of mass destruction?
Mesopotamia has no chemical weapons
Mesopotamia has no biological
weapons *but Mesopotamia has oil!*

Prologue

"According to the United Nations, "...climate change refers to long term shifts in temperatures and weather patterns. These shifts may be natural, but since the 1800s, human activities have been the main driver of climate change, primarily due to the burning of fossil fuels (like coal, oil, and gas) which produce heat-trapping gases."

An Inconvenient Truth

1.5 degrees Celsius
a point of no return
outlined in *Paris Agreement* (1)
facts light the
corners of your mind
illuminate the inner
recesses of our comprehension
climate change encroaching
affecting developed
and developing world alike
climate change does not discriminate
Africa, Antarctica
Asia, Australia
North America, South America
and Europe
coral bleaching is intensifying
climate change accelerating
sea levels encroaching
climate change overwhelming
flash flooding humdrum
climate change overwhelming
weather events transmogrifying
cyclones intensifying
categories 4 and 5 hurricanes
climate change launching
breakneck twisters
EF 4 and *EF 5* tropical storms

climate change igniting
wildfires blowing up
winds suddenly changing direction
fires too intense to overrun
why do climate deniers get the press
when *An Inconvenient
Truth*
is obvious to all

Prologue

Libation is a drink poured to the ground as an offering to a deity. In West Africa, libation is poured to honor the memory of the deceased. In Ghana and Africa in general, ancestors are an intermediary between the living and the dead. During the "Middle Passage," many captives would have invoked the spirits of the ancestors for intervention.

Pour Libation

in the misty dew of a chilly
harmattan morning in
December of the year 1762
talking drums wailed to
announce another raid
by unscrupulous slave captors
families frantically searched
for missing loved ones
a week earlier, the local ruler
King Nii Tackie and his wife
Queen Mother Naa Amanua
had organized a welcoming party
for his guests as was customary
the guests had turned out
to be slave captors
King Nii Tackie had even slaughtered
goats and cattle
in the town of Ngleshie
(Jamestown, British Accra)
holding a banquet for guests
was regarded as a sign of respect
one of the captured town's folks
turned out to be the king's son
Nii Seeku
the prince silently prayed
that his father would send a rescue party
which the noble king did

unfortunately, the rescue party
could not locate the captured group
presently, Nii Seeku wondered
who would inform his new bride
Naa Lamle that he had been whisked
to a faraway land
who would tell Naadu, his mother
and future regent that he had not forsaken
his position as future king
who would inform the spirit of
his deceased father, Owula Quao
that Nii Seeku had not been derelict
as a future king
who would tell Nii Gbeto, Naa Okailey
and Naa Okaikor, that Nii Seeku
had not forgotten his responsibility
as the eldest son
who would tell Uncle Sas
and Uncle Nii Sampa, the kingmakers
that Nii Seeku could not fulfill his duties
because Nii Seeku had been captured
presently
Nii Seeku spotted Father Steven
laboring up a promontory
a week earlier, Father Steven had
informed Nii Seeku that Jesus
was the only way, the truth
and the light

Father Steven assured that
God regarded all men as equals
so why then was Nii Seeku
a future king
being used as chattel?
a familiar mix of salty sea spray
and seaweed awakened Nii Seeku
from his reverie
meanwhile, the faint outlines
of the fabled Osu slave castle
came into focus
at that moment, Nii Seeku's eyes
widened in horror as he recalled
the prophecy of the old and wrinkled
fortune teller
Nii Seeku's destiny could not be fulfilled
in his hometown of Ngleshie
Nii Seeku's destiny would be fulfilled
in distant shores
Okyeame (family elder)
pour libation
and tell my ancestors to receive my chi
Okyeame
pour libation and ask my
deceased father to come for me
Okyeame
pour libation and assure my ancestors
that I am dead to this town

References

https://www.americaspace.com/2023/02/01/lock-the-doors-remembering-columbias-final-return-home-twenty-years-on/#:~:text=Seconds%20later%2C%20at%208:59,Photo%20Credit:%20NASA

www.ingramcontent.com/pod-product-compliance
Lightning Source LLC
Chambersburg PA
CBHW031658040426
42453CB00006B/338